Vacation
Bible
Splash

BARBOUR
PUBLISHING, INC.
Uhrichsville, Ohio

Published by Barbour Publishing, Inc., P.O. Box 719, Uhrichsville, OH 44683 http://www.barbourbooks.com

ecpa Member of the
Evangelical Christian
Publishers Association

Printed in the United States of America.

INTRODUCTION

It's summer—time to do and go! With classes out (and nothing to slow you down), you'll take trips to the beach, the amusement park, the baseball stadium, and a hundred other destinations. Why not include a tour of your Bible?

Welcome to *Vacation Bible Splash*, your ticket to Bible fun this summer. From Genesis to Revelation, this book will be your guide to the greatest Book of all time—your Bible. Packed with fun puzzles, word games, and jokes, *Vacation Bible Splash* is the perfect companion for those long, fun-filled days of summer. Dive on in!

"Who was the fastest runner in history?" asked Shelley.

"Adam," said Mackie. "The Bible says he was first in the human race."

Old Testament Word Find

Read over the list of names of the books of the Old Testament, then try this puzzle:

All of the books of the Old Testament are in the word find on the next page. Books that have two parts are listed once (Samuel, Kings, and Chronicles) so that you will find a total of 36 different titles. Song of Solomon is listed here as Song of Songs. Use your Bible's index for a list of all the books.

Words may be across, down, upside down, or backwards. There are no diagonals.

```
P S Q G E N E S I S D J O N A H
S G W C L E I K E Z E M U H A N
A N E H S B O J L E U M A S Y Z
L I Z R N X Z O A P T P V J E E
M K R O O Z X S M H E R S O C C
S D A N I E L H O A R O R E C H
L E V I T I C U S N O V E L L A
J Q J C A G P A X I N E B W E R
E M U L T R U T H A O R M H S I
R A D E N M I C A H M B U A I A
E L G S E S T H E R Y S N I A H
M A E Q M Q X E X O D U S D S O
I C S H A B A K K U K L L A T S
A H Y G L H A G G A I W Q B E E
H I M M S G N O S F O G N O S A
N E H E M I A H X I S A I A H Q
```

The Creation
and the Fall
Genesis 1–10

1) Who wrote the book of Genesis?

2) What did God do on the first day?

3) What three things did God create on the
    fourth day to light the universe?

4) Did you know that gold and onyx could be
    found in the Garden of Eden? (Genesis 2:12)

5) Why did Eden have a river running through it?

6) The name of the first man was:
    a) Abraham   c) Joseph
    b) Noah   d) Adam

7) Who named all of the living creatures?

8) Why did God decide to create a woman?

9) The name of the first woman was:
    a) Evelyn   c) Eve
    b) Rachel   d) Rebekah

10) Did you know that the first woman's name
    means mother of all living? (Genesis 3:20)

11) What did God take from Adam to make Eve?

12) Did you know that Adam and Eve were the
    first married couple? (Genesis 2:23–24)

13) The first woman was tempted by a:
    a) serpent   c) dinosaur
    b) ladybug   d) spider

14) If Eve would eat the forbidden fruit, the serpent promised her:
    a) clothing
    b) riches
    c) a starring role in a movie
    d) knowledge of good and evil

15) Did you know that Moses wrote the first five books of the Bible?

16) After discovering their nakedness, how did Adam and Eve clothe themselves?

17) What did Adam and Eve do when they heard God calling?

18) When he was caught disobeying God, Adam blamed:
    a) the serpent
    b) bad programs on television
    c) Cain
    d) Eve

19) After Adam and Eve ate the forbidden fruit, God:
    a) sent them out of Eden
    b) let them stay in Eden
    c) poured manna from heaven
    d) told them to build an ark so he could begin the human race again

20) Whom did God put in place to guard the tree of life?

Adam and Eve
Genesis 2:7-3:21

ACROSS
1) Eve's name means "The _____ of all living."

2) What was the name of the garden?

3) What did Adam and Eve eat from?

DOWN
1) What was Adam made from?

2) Who tempted Eve?

3) What did God clothe Adam and Eve with?

Adam and Eve's Sons
Genesis 4:1-25

ACROSS
1) Able was Adam and Eve's _____ born son.

2) What did Cain do for a living?

3) What was the name of Adam's third son?

DOWN
1) What did Abel do for a living?

2) Cain was Adam and Eve's _____ born son.

3) The Lord looked on Abel with favor because of his _____.

The First Murder—
The Flood
Genesis 4-10

1) Who was the first son of Adam and Eve?

2) Who was the second son born to Adam and Eve?

3) Did you know that the slaying of Abel by Cain was the first murder?

4) When Cain went out of the Lord's presence, he went to live in:
   - a) Mod
   - b) Nod
   - c) Sod
   - d) Cod

5) Did you know that John Steinbeck wrote a book called *East of Eden?* This is also where Cain went to live after being exiled. (Genesis 4:16)

6) Who was Cain and Abel's brother?

7) Who was Methuselah's father?

8) What is mentioned twice about Enoch?

9) Methuselah lived how many years?
   - a) 30
   - b) 69
   - c) 90
   - d) 969

10) God told Noah to build:
   a) a yacht for Christian cruises
   b) an airplane
   c) an ark
   d) a tugboat

11) Did you know that a cubit measures 18 inches long?

12) How old was Noah when the flood began?

13) One of Noah's sons was named:
   a) Ham   c) Salami
   b) Sham   d) Pastrami

14) Did you know that Noah's ark was 450 feet long?

What did Noah do for a living?
He was an ark-itect.

Did It Ever Rain!

Read the story of Noah and the flood in Genesis 6:9–9:17. Then answer the questions. Choose your answers from the words below. Some words and numbers will not be used.

1) Noah was a _____ man.

2) God said, "Make yourself an ark of _____ wood."

3) "I am going to bring _____ on the earth to destroy all life," said God.

4) Noah was _____ years old when the flood came.

5) He took his _____ into the ark with him.

6) He also took his _____ sons and their _____ into the ark.

7) It rained for _____ days and nights.

8) Noah's sons were named _____, _____, and _____.

9) God sent a _____ over the earth and the waters receded.

10) Noah sent a _____ out of the ark.

WORD LIST

cypress	wind	dove	floodwaters	40
Ham	Japheth	Reuben	righteous	wives
70	Shem	600	sons	three
two	200			wife

12

The Flood
Genesis 7:10–8:8

ACROSS
1) How many days was Noah on the ark before the flood waters came?

2) How many days and nights did it rain?

3) What kind of bird did Noah send out of the ark the second time?

DOWN
1) How many people were on the ark?

2) How many of each living creature went on the ark?

3) What kind of bird did Noah sent out of the ark the first time?

A New World
Genesis 11–50

1) To reach heaven, the people tried to build:
   a) the Empire State Building
   b) a highway to heaven
   c) the Tower of Babel
   d) the Sears Building

2) What did the Lord do when He discovered that men were trying to build a tower to reach heaven?

3) What land did Lot choose for himself when he and Abram separated?

4) Did you know that Mohammed, the founder of the religion of Islam, was from the line of Ishmael?

5) Hagar was:
   a) the mother of Ishmael
   b) the founder of the Haggar Clothing Company
   c) the mother of Abraham
   d) Sarah's neighbor

6) When Ishmael was born, his father Abram was age:
   a) 26   c) 86
   b) 36   d) 96

7) Abram's name was changed to:
   a) Lot   c) Bam-Bam
   b) Abraham   d) Brahma

8) Why did God change Abram's name to Abraham?

9) Did you know that the Hebrew word "Shaddai" is the name used for God most often in the Bible's early books? Did you know that Shaddai means "All Sufficient" or "Almighty"?

10) Who wrote the first five books of the Bible?

11) When God promised Abraham that his wife Sarah would have a baby, he:
    a) praised God
    b) invested in a college fund
    c) bought a box of expensive cigars
    d) laughed

12) Why did Abraham give God such a response to the news?

13) God destroyed the evil cities of:
    a) Sodom and Gomorrah
    b) Bethlehem and Nazareth
    c) London and Paris
    d) Bug Tussle and Navel Lint

14) What happened to Lot's wife when she looked back at the cities?

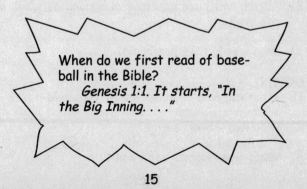

When do we first read of baseball in the Bible?
    Genesis 1:1. It starts, "In the Big Inning. . . ."

Abram
Genesis 12:5–16:15

ACROSS
1) What relation was Abram to Lot?

2) Abram will have as many offspring as what in the sky?

3) Who was Sarai's handmaid?

DOWN
1) What did God promise Abram he would have?

2) Who was Abram's wife?

3) What was Hagar's son's name?

The Promise and the Test
Genesis 21:3–22:17

WHEW!!

ACROSS

1) What does Isaac's name mean?

2) How many servants went with Abraham?

3) Who stopped Abraham from sacrificing Isaac?

DOWN

1) Who was Abraham and Sarah's son?

2) Abraham was going to _____ Isaac on the mountain.

3) God was _____ Abraham when He asked him to sacrifice Isaac.

The Blessing

Genesis 45:3-50:26

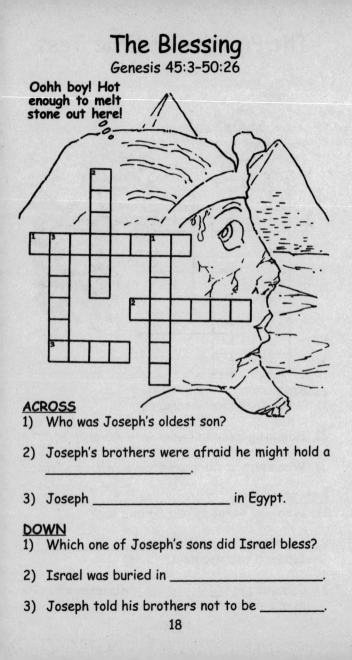

Oohh boy! Hot enough to melt stone out here!

ACROSS
1) Who was Joseph's oldest son?

2) Joseph's brothers were afraid he might hold a

_____.

3) Joseph _____ in Egypt.

DOWN
1) Which one of Joseph's sons did Israel bless?

2) Israel was buried in _____.

3) Joseph told his brothers not to be _____.

Batting 1,000

Total your answers to the following questions. If you are correct, your total should be 1,000!

1) Adam was the first man. Turn to Genesis 5:5 to find out how old he was when he died.

   Answer _____

2) How many people entered Noah's ark to escape the great flood? Look at Genesis 7:13.

   Answer _____

3) Before the tower of Babel, how many different languages were in the world? Genesis 11:1

   Answer _____

4) How many brothers did Joseph have? Genesis 37:9. Hint: He saw his brothers as stars in a dream.

   Answer _____

5) How many chapters are there in the book of Genesis?

   Answer _____

Now total your answers: _____

If you hit 1,000, you are the champion!

Strongman Samson
Judges 13–16

1) Did you know that an angel appeared to Samson's mother before his birth and told her that his hair was not to be cut?

2) The angel also told Samson's mother not to drink:
   - a) 7-up
   - b) manna
   - c) water from the creek
   - d) wine or strong drink

3) The angel also appeared before:
   - a) Samson's father Manoah
   - b) Noah
   - c) Herman Munster
   - d) Fred Flintstone

4) What was the angel's name?

5) The woman Samson wanted to marry was a:
   - a) Jewess
   - b) Hollywood star
   - c) U.S. citizen
   - d) Philistine

6) When a lion attacked Samson after he visited the woman, he:
   - a) killed it with his bare hands
   - b) killed it with a slingshot
   - c) made it his pet and named it Delilah
   - d) ran over it with his car

7) Inside the lion's carcass, Samson found:
   - a) the sword Excalibur
   - b) raspberry flavored spring water
   - c) a swarm of bees and honey
   - d) granola bars

8) What did Samson challenge his wedding banquet guests to do?

9) The answer was given away by:
   a) an angel   c) Samson's mother
   b) Samson's wife   d) the TV news

10) Because she thought Samson hated her, after the feast Samson's wife married:
   a) Samson's friend   c) Adam
   b) Abraham   d) Michael Card

11) Samson killed a thousand Philistines with a:
   a) dog's tail
   b) bucket of cream pies
   c) bb gun
   d) donkey's jawbone

12) What did Samson do to make good on his promise to give thirty people fine cloaks?

13) After the battle, God gave Samson water from:
   a) a rock
   b) the Old Faithful geyser at Yellowstone National Park
   c) a vending machine that appeared inside of a burning bush
   d) the donkey's jawbone

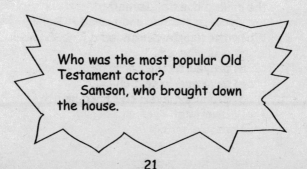

Who was the most popular Old Testament actor?
    Samson, who brought down the house.

From Judges to a King
I Samuel 8-10

1) Did you know that God's people were under a government called a theocracy? That means they were ruled by God.

2) When Samuel got old, he:
    a) married a young woman
    b) made his sons judges in his place
    c) had to take antacid after every meal
    d) refused to stop judging Israel

3) The people were unhappy with Samuel's sons because they:
    a) took bribes and did not rule fairly
    b) did not exercise
    c) had promised free education for all and then didn't build any schools
    d) had not kept their promise of giving everyone a chicken in every pot

4) What were the names of Samuel's two sons?

5) Had Samuel been a good judge?

6) Did you know that Samuel was the last of the true judges of Israel?

7) When the people demanded a king, Samuel:
    a) was pleased
    b) prayed to the Lord
    c) gave everyone a chicken
    d) promised everyone free health benefits

8) The Lord told Samuel to:
   a) let the people see how a king would rule
   b) sacrifice two goats and a perfect male ram
   c) produce two more sons more worthy to be judges
   d) store grain for seven years because there would be seven years of famine

9) When the people asked for a king, whom did the Lord say they were really rejecting?

10) Samuel warned the people that a king would be:
    a) greedy
    b) a blessing to the nation
    c) as brilliant as Albert Einstein
    d) as rich as Bill Gates

11) Did the people heed Samuel's warning?

12) What was the name of Israel's first king?

13) Did you know that Saul was a descendant of the tribe of Benjamin? Saul's father was Kish; his grandfather was Abiel; his great-grandfather was Zeror, and his great-great grandfather was a powerful Benjamite named Aphiah.

14) Saul was known for:
    a) owning a red monster truck
    b) winning the pie eating contest at the state fair five years in a row
    c) being the shortest and ugliest man in all of Israel
    d) being the tallest and most handsome man in all of Israel

Young Blood
I Samuel 15-17

1) Why did God reject Saul as king?

2) Did you know that God sent Samuel to Bethlehem, the city of Jesus' birth, to find the next king? (I Samuel 16:4)

3) Samuel thought that Eliab should be the second king because Eliab was:
   a) handsome
   b) rich
   c) planning to give Samuel money for his ministry
   d) good

4) The Lord told Samuel that people see outward beauty, but He sees their:
   a) intelligence
   b) possessions
   c) time put in at Bible study class
   d) hearts

5) Who was the future king's father?

6) How many sons did Samuel see before he saw the future king?

7) David was:
   a) short and slightly pudgy
   b) glowing with health and handsome to look at
   c) quarterback on the football team
   d) a brainy person who wore thick glasses

8) What did the Lord tell Samuel to do when Samuel saw David?

9) Why did Saul want to be soothed by music?

10) David was skillful at playing the:
    a) electric organ   c) accordion
    b) kazoo   d) harp

11) Who was to be the new king of Israel?

12) In Saul's court, David:
    a) loved Saul and became his armor-bearer
    b) hated Saul because David wanted to
       be king right away
    c) became Saul's food taster
    d) was thrown into a lion's den

13) Who was Goliath?

14) Did you know that Goliath's height measured
    six cubits and a span? A cubit measures about
    21 inches, while a span measures the length of
    three palms of a man's hand. This means that
    Goliath was somewhere between 9 and 11 feet
    tall. (I Samuel 17:4)

15) Which of David's brothers went with Saul to
    battle the Philistines?

What did Noah say when he'd
finished loading the ark?
     *"Now I've herded every-
thing."*

Talking With God:
The Psalms

ACROSS

1) David _____ God in the Psalms.

2) David _____ to his sins in the Psalms.

3) David expressed his _____ for God in the Psalms.

DOWN

1) David was known as a man after God's own _____.

2) David shared his _____ in the Psalms with God.

3) David used the Psalms to _____ to God.

Majestic Is His Name
Psalm 8

ACROSS
1) "You have set your glory above the _____."

2) "What is man that you are _____ of him."

3) "O Lord, our _____."

DOWN
1) "You made _____ ruler over the works of your hands."

2) "You have ordained _____."

3) "How majestic is your _____."

David's Psalm

David wrote the 23rd Psalm, which is one of the most famous parts of the Bible. Fill in the missing words to complete the Psalm. Use your Bible to find the answers from the words at the bottom of the page. All the words will be used.

The Lord is my _____, I shall not be in want. He makes me lie down in _____ _____, he _____ me beside quiet _____, he restores my _____. He guides me in paths of _____ for his name's sake. Even though I walk through the _____ of the _____ of death, I will _____ no evil, for you are with me; your _____ and your _____, they comfort me. You prepare a table before me in the presence of my enemies. You anoint my _____ with oil; my _____ overflows. Surely goodness and _____ will follow me all the days of my life, and I will dwell in the _____ of the Lord _____.

Word List

cup	fear	forever	green
head	house	leads	love
pastures	shadow	shepherd	soul
staff	valley	waters	rod
righteousness			

28

You, Lord, Are My Salvation

Psalm 27:1-6

ACROSS

1) "The Lord is the _____ of my life."

2) "To gaze upon the beauty of the _____."

3) "I _____ sing and make music to the Lord."

DOWN

1) "The Lord is my light and my _____."

2) " _____ thing I ask of the Lord."

3) "That I may _____ in the house of the Lord."

You, Lord, Are
Forgiving and Good

Psalm 86:5-11

ACROSS

1) "You are _____ and good."

2) "And I will _____ in your truth."

3) "Give me an undivided _____."

DOWN

1) "_____ in love to all who call to you."

2) "Teach me _____ way."

3) "That I may _____ your name."

31

With God
I Will Have Victory
Psalm 108:4-13

ACROSS

1) "Your faithfulness reaches to the _____ ."

2) "Give us aid against the _____ ."

3) "And He will _____ down our enemies."

DOWN

1) "For great is your _____ ."

2) "Be exalted, O God, above the _____ ."

3) "With God we will gain the _____ ."

I Will Make Music to The Lord

Psalm 150:3-6

ACROSS

1) "Praise Him with the harp and _____."

2) "Praise Him with the _____ of cymbals."

3) "Let everything that has _____, praise the Lord."

DOWN

1) "Praise Him with the sounding of the _____ ."

2) "Praise _____ with tambourine and dancing."

3) "Praise Him with the strings and _____."

Proverbs

Turn to Proverbs, the book that comes after Psalms. Remember that Psalms is in the center of your Bible. Solve the coded puzzle below to find out what you can have by reading this book.

$$\overline{4}\ \overline{8}\ \overline{1}$$

$$\overline{6}\ \overline{13}\ \overline{5}\ \overline{11}\ \overline{2}\ \overline{10}$$

$$\overline{2}\ \overline{7}\qquad \overline{3}\ \overline{13}\ \overline{9}\ \overline{12}$$

$$\overline{5}\ \overline{2}\ \overline{14}\ \overline{2}\ \overline{10}\ \overline{2}\ \overline{9}$$

Key

1 = E	5 = S	9 = N	13 = I
2 = O	6 = W	10 = M	14 = L
3 = K	7 = F	11 = D	
4 = T	8 = H	12 = G	

Shelby: "Do you know at what point in history God created Eve?"

Sandra: "Right after He created Adam."

Bits of Wisdom
Proverbs

1) Solomon was:
    a) a king of Israel
    b) one of the twelve disciples
    c) David's father
    d) a writer for popular TV programs

2) Who is the giver of wisdom?

3) A wise person runs away from:
    a) a pesky younger brother
    b) chores
    c) Dad when there's a bad report card
    d) evil

4) When the Lord loves you, He:
    a) shows you right from wrong
    b) gives you money beyond your dreams
    c) won't let you get chicken pox
    d) will make sure your homework gets done

5) Happy is the person who finds what?

6) We should be like ants because they:
    a) work   c) are pretty
    b) steal picnic food   d) are quiet

7) Proverbs lists how many things that the Lord hates?
    a) six   c) sixty-six
    b) seven   d) seventeen

8) Proverbs cautions against:
    a) having too many wives
    b) bad women
    c) letting women take you to a boring party
    d) letting your wife have her way

9) Did you know that the book of Proverbs was put together in the tenth century before Christ?

10) You should think of wisdom as your:
    a) mother   c) fiancée
    b) daughter   d) sister

11) Did you know that when the author of Proverbs says to call wisdom your sister, it means that you should hold wisdom in high regard? You can also think of it as walking hand in hand with wisdom, a cherished virtue.

12) Wisdom is better than:
    a) cherry bubble gum
    b) winning the lottery
    c) rubies
    d) the prizes in happy meals

13) Who wrote the book of Proverbs?

14) Did you know that a proverb is a wise saying?

15) What is the theme of the book of Proverbs?

16) When you tell a wise person about a mistake, the person will:
    a) laugh at you   c) hate you
    b) love you   d) gossip about you

17) Why does a wise person welcome correction?

18) According to Proverbs, will wisdom make you live longer?

19) Hatred stirs anger, but sin is covered by:
    a) hate   c) love
    b) anger   d) slime

20) Does the book of Proverbs advise against gossip?

21) Why do you think the author of Proverbs would say not to speak badly of others?

22) A person who will not listen to wise advice will find:
   a) poverty and shame
   b) health and wealth
   c) his own wisdom
   d) a walk-on part on "Saved by the Bell"

23) A person who heeds wise advice will find:
   a) shame
   b) a winning lottery ticket
   c) honor
   d) fame

24) What can you do to make someone less angry?

25) Pleasant words are like a:
   a) sword
   b) spear
   c) sweet potato pie
   d) honeycomb

26) What is the crown of an old man?

27) According to Proverbs, we will be punished if we:
   a) tell lies
   b) beat up the school bully
   c) spend too much time playing computer games
   d) make bad grades in school

28) Did you know that even a child will be known by his actions? (Proverbs 20:11)

29) What does Proverbs 20:23 mean by saying dishonest scales do not please Him?

How Can I Make Wise Choices: The Proverbs

Proverbs 1:2-7

ACROSS

1) "For attaining wisdom and _____."

2) "Doing what is right and _____ and fair."

3) "The _____ of the Lord."

DOWN

1) "For understanding words of
   _____ ."

2) "Let the wise _____."

3) "Is the_____ of knowledge."

Sunday School Teacher: "Who was Noah's
    wife?"
Student: "Er . . . Joan of Ark?"

Wisdom Will Save Me

Proverbs 2:6-12

ACROSS

1) "For the Lord _____ wisdom."

2) "From His _____."

3) "And _____ will guard you."

DOWN

1) "_____ will be pleasant to your soul."

2) "For wisdom will _____ your heart."

3) "Wisdom will save you from the ways of _____ men."

A Good Name
Proverbs 3:4-6

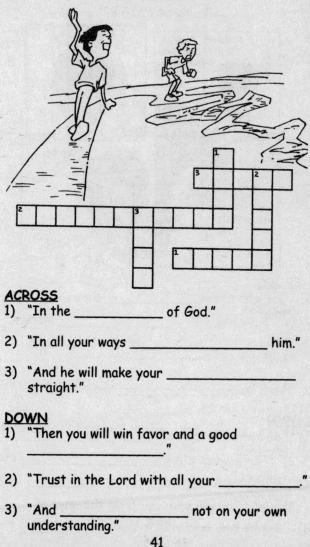

ACROSS

1) "In the _____ of God."

2) "In all your ways _____ him."

3) "And he will make your _____ straight."

DOWN

1) "Then you will win favor and a good _____."

2) "Trust in the Lord with all your _____."

3) "And _____ not on your own understanding."

41

The Blessing of the Lord

Proverbs 10:17-22

ACROSS

1) "He who heeds _____ shows the way to life."

2) "The _____ of the Lord brings wealth."

3) "And he _____ no trouble to it."

DOWN

1) "And whoever spreads _____ is a fool."

2) "When words are many, _____ is not absent."

3) "But he who holds his tongue is _____."

43

The Good Wife
Proverbs, Chapter 31

1) A good woman is:
   - a) noble
   - b) beautiful
   - c) rich
   - d) skinny

2) What is a virtue?

3) A good woman is more valuable than what?

4) Her husband can trust his wife with his:
   - a) pet hamster
   - b) credit cards
   - c) full confidence
   - d) car

5) What two things does the Proverbs 31 woman select?

6) Who gives honor to the good wife?

7) When it is time to work, she:
   - a) passes off her chores to her children
   - b) hires the best maid in town
   - c) works willingly
   - d) calls her mother on the phone and complains

8) Where does the Proverbs 31 woman get food?

9) The Proverbs 31 woman starts her day:
   - a) before dawn
   - b) after she's caught up on all the latest gossip
   - c) noon
   - d) as soon as her children get in from school

10) What virtue is described in Proverbs 31:14-19?

11) The virtue of giving to the poor is called:
    a) flattery   c) guile
    b) deceit   d) charity

12) She is not afraid of snow because:
    a) it gives her a chance to rent videos and eat microwave popcorn all day
    b) she has plenty of clothing to keep her family warm
    c) she has a four-wheel-drive vehicle
    d) the central heating system in her house is always working

13) What color does the Proverbs 31 woman wear?

14) Did you know that purple was once worn only by very rich people? In Bible times, purple dye came from a shellfish that could only produce a little color at a time, so the dye was very expensive.

15) What does the virtuous woman sell?

16) A good wife wears:
    a) a frown on her face
    b) plenty of red lipstick
    c) only the latest sneakers
    d) strength and dignity

17) When a good woman speaks, what do her words have?

18) Beauty is not the first concern of the Proverbs 31 woman because she:
    a) already sold her stock in Revlon
    b) is too old to be a model
    c) is not vain or conceited
    d) is vain and conceited

Dream Weaver
Daniel

1) Who wrote the book of Daniel?

2) Did you know that the book of Daniel is called an apocalypse? Apocalypse means "unveiling." The book of Daniel shows that good will win over evil.

3) When Daniel had a chance to eat the rich foods of King Nebuchadnezzar, he asked:
   a) for second helpings
   b) for a doggy bag
   c) for Pharoah's own steak sauce for his beef Wellington
   d) to be excused from eating food forbidden under Jewish dietary laws

4) When the Lord heard Daniel's request not to eat the king's food, what did the Lord grant Daniel?

5) What special talent did God give to Daniel that would later help the king?

6) Did you know that the book of Daniel was written in the Aramaic language?

7) What did King Nebuchadnezzar say should happen to his wise men when they couldn't interpret his dream?

8) King Nebuchadnezzar made an image of what kind of metal?

9) Did you know that the image King Nebuchadnezzar made was 90 feet high? (Daniel 3:1)

10) When King Nebuchadnezzar asked Daniel to interpret his dream, Daniel:
   a) asked the king for more time and prayed to God for wisdom
   b) told the king about the dream right away
   c) asked for more of the king's rich food
   d) presented him with a contract asking for blue M&M candies

11) Anyone who refused to worship the image would be:
   a) honored by King Nebuchadnezzar
   b) granted the king's daughter's hand in marriage
   c) thrown into a fiery furnace
   d) given extra money to buy Warheads candy

12) After the king dreamed of a tree, he:
   a) went to live with the beasts of the field, eating grass for food
   b) became a forest ranger for the U.S. Park Service
   c) walked around the country with a pot on his head, planting apple seeds
   d) ate wild locusts and honey

13) Did you know that the king had given Daniel the name Belteshazzar? (Daniel 5:12)

14) What did King Belshazzar do at his banquet to offend God?

15) God communicated to King Belshazzar:
   a) with handwriting on a wall
   b) through a burning bush
   c) through the U.S. Post Office
   d) by appearing on TV

The Unwilling Servant
Jonah

1) Who wrote the book of Jonah?

2) Did you know that Jonah was the first foreign missionary?

3) Where did God tell Jonah to go?

4) Jonah went to:
   - a) Nineveh
   - b) Tarshish
   - c) Joppa
   - d) Cleveland

5) Jonah tried to hide:
   - a) on The Love Boat
   - b) on a ship heading to Tarshish
   - c) at the home of Johnny Quest
   - d) under his bed

6) Did you know that the name "Jonah" means "Dove"?

7) What did God send out that frightened the people on the ship?

8) As Jonah slept on the ship, the others called out to:
   - a) their gods
   - b) Jehovah
   - c) a UFO they spotted
   - d) a news van from a local TV station

9) Did they throw Jonah overboard right away?

10) Did you know that the Bible does not say that Jonah was swallowed by a whale, but a great fish? (Jonah 1:17)

11) Since he had put them in danger, Jonah told the others to:
   a) be sure they had plenty of food
   b) interpret his dream from the night before
   c) convert to Jonah's faith
   d) throw him overboard

12) After Jonah was thrown overboard, the sea:
   a) grew even rougher
   b) made big waves for the surf dudes to ride
   c) parted
   d) grew calm

13) What did Jonah do while he was inside the fish?

14) After the fish vomited Jonah onto dry land, the Lord told Jonah to:
   a) take a bath
   b) go to Nineveh
   c) return home
   d) apologize to the men on the ship

15) Did you know that the city of Nineveh was so large that it took three days to walk all the way around it? (Jonah 3:3)

16) How long was Jonah inside the fish?

17) What was Jonah's message to Nineveh from God?

18) Upon hearing the message, the people of Nineveh:
   a) fasted and wore sackcloth
   b) ate a big turkey dinner
   c) ate only chocolate and wore only purple for three days
   d) celebrated Lent

The 39 Books

There are 39 books in the Old Testament. Can you name them in the correct order?

1) _____   21) _____
2) _____   22) _____
3) _____   23) _____
4) _____   24) _____
5) _____   25) _____
6) _____   26) _____
7) _____   27) _____
8) _____   28) _____
9) _____   29) _____
10) _____   30) _____
11) _____   31) _____
12) _____   32) _____
13) _____   33) _____
14) _____   34) _____
15) _____   35) _____
16) _____   36) _____
17) _____   37) _____
18) _____   38) _____
19) _____   39) _____
20) _____

Look in the front of your Bible
for the answers!

Animal Crackers

The name of an animal or bird found in the Bible is hidden in each line of the puzzle below. Each name will use the dark letter in the center of the line. That letter can be found in any part of the word. A sample has been done for you.

F	B	E	A	R	E	N
B	R	A	B	B	I	T
M	J	A	C	K	A	L
L	A	S	D	O	G	P
V	S	H	E	O	P	O
G	R	E	F	R	O	G
C	E	A	G	L	E	N
P	S	T	H	A	R	E
B	L	P	I	G	N	I
			J			
C	O	C	K	E	R	G
S	M	O	L	E	N	A
T	R	E	M	O	T	H
L	I	O	N	B	R	O
D	U	G	O	A	T	L
L	E	O	P	A	R	D
			Q			
S	P	A	R	R	O	W
M	O	U	S	E	A	C
R	B	A	T	E	L	V
M	O	Q	U	A	I	L
G	D	O	V	E	L	I
S	N	O	W	L	E	R
T	F	O	X	E	N	Z
			Y			
S	L	I	Z	A	R	D

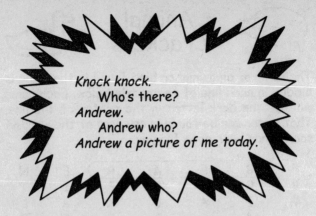

Knock knock.
Who's there?
Andrew.
Andrew who?
Andrew a picture of me today.

New
Testament
Word Find

Just like the Old Testament, the books of the New Testament are in the same order in every Bible. You will find a list of New Testament books either at the beginning of the New Testament in your Bible, or at the front of your Bible after the Old Testament books.

See if you can find all the books of the New Testament. Books with a I, II, or III in front of them are listed only once, so there are a total of 21 titles to look for.

Words may be across, down, upside down, or backwards. There are no diagonals.

```
T R E V E L A T I O N S S
H E B R E W S J U D E R T
E P H E S I A N S J O O C
S E T I J O H N M A Q M O
S T I M O T H Y A M V A R
A E T Q H P R W R E N N I
L R U O N T R W K S L S N
O J S A C T S L U K E V T
N U G A L A T I A N S M H
I D M A T T H E W L K L I
A C O L O S S I A N S Q A
N P H I L E M O N V B Z N
S K P H I L I P P I A N S
```

Matthew's Gospel
Matthew

1) Who wrote the book of Matthew?

2) Did you know that Matthew was a tax collector?

3) The book of Matthew starts by recording:
   a) Jesus' birth   c) St. Paul's birth
   b) the creation   d) Jesus' birth line,
                                 or genealogy

4) Did you know that it was unusual for birth records to mention women, although Matthew mentions them in his gospel?

5) In what city was Jesus born?

6) Did you know that the King Herod of Jesus' time was known as Herod the Great?

7) King Herod sought the baby Jesus to:
   a) worship Him
   b) give Him gold, frankincense, and myrrh
   c) give Mary and Joseph money for a hotel room at Embassy Suites
   d) kill Him

8) To keep Him safe from Herod, Mary and Joseph took Jesus to:
   a) Egypt   c)   Edom
   b) Uz   d)   Paris

9) The food John the Baptist ate was:
   a) manna
   b) cookies made by elves
   c) milk and honey
   d) locusts and wild honey

10) Did you know that all of the Gospels record the ministry of John the Baptist?

11) How long was Jesus tempted by the devil?

12) What would Peter and Andrew fish for if they followed Jesus?

13) Another name for Jesus' Sermon on the Mount is:
   a) Beatitudes
   b) Attitude Adjustments
   c) Beatniks
   d) Assertiveness Training

14) Did you know that the comparisons of Christians to salt and light are called Similitudes?

15) What do we call the prayer Jesus taught His disciples?

16) Jesus said to store your treasures in:
   a) the stock market   c) real estate
   b) mutual funds   d) heaven

17) Did you know that in New Testament times, a worker earned about sixteen cents a day?

18) What do we call Jesus' command to do unto others as you would have them to unto you?

19) The relative of Peter's whom Jesus healed was Peter's:
   a) second cousin twice removed
   b) kissin' cousin
   c) step-great-grandmother
   d) mother-in-law

20) What is another name for the stories Jesus used to teach people?

21) How many disciples did Jesus call?

22) When the disciples saw Jesus walking on the water, they thought He was a:
    a) ghost   c)   hallucination
    b) hologram   d)   mirage

23) Jesus healed the Canaanite woman's daughter because of her:
    a) great faith
    b) gifts of gold, frankincense, and myrrh
    c) desire to wash His feet with perfume
    d) gift of a video game set and several cartridges

24) Did Jesus know He was to be crucified?

25) We should be watchful because:
    a) someone might steal our treasures
    b) we don't know when the Lord will return
    c) we might have forgotten to turn on our security systems
    d) our watchdog is at the vet

26) Which disciple agreed to betray Jesus?

27) Jesus was betrayed in exchange for:
    a) nothing
    b) tickets to a concert
    c) the widow's mite
    d) thirty pieces of silver

28) What was the name of the garden where Jesus prayed before His crucifixion?

A Parable: The Lost Sheep

Matthew 18:12-13

ACROSS

1) "If a man owns a _____ sheep."

2) "And go to _____ for the one that wandered off."

3) "I _____ you the truth."

DOWN

1) "Will he not leave the ninety-nine on the _____."

2) "And one of them _____ away."

3) "And if he _____ it."

I Was Lost, But Now I'm Found

Matthew 18:13-14

ACROSS

1) "Than about the ninety-nine that did not
   _____ off."

2) "Your Father in _____."

3) "That any of these little _____
   should be lost."

DOWN

1) "He is happier about that one _____."

2) "In the same _____."

3) "Is _____ willing."

Read The Dial

Decide which letters on the telephone buttons you will use to decode the message below. Need a hint? Check out Matthew 25:21. This one's a challenge!

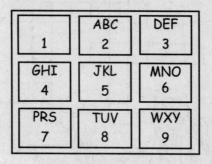

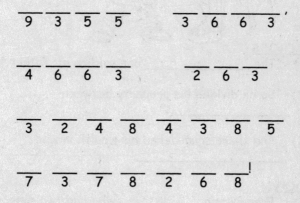

$\overline{9}\ \overline{3}\ \overline{5}\ \overline{5}$ $\overline{3}\ \overline{6}\ \overline{6}\ \overline{3}$'

$\overline{4}\ \overline{6}\ \overline{6}\ \overline{3}$ $\overline{2}\ \overline{6}\ \overline{3}$

$\overline{3}\ \overline{2}\ \overline{4}\ \overline{8}\ \overline{4}\ \overline{3}\ \overline{8}\ \overline{5}$

$\overline{7}\ \overline{3}\ \overline{7}\ \overline{8}\ \overline{2}\ \overline{6}\ \overline{8}$!

A Parable:
The Lost Son
Luke 15:11-13

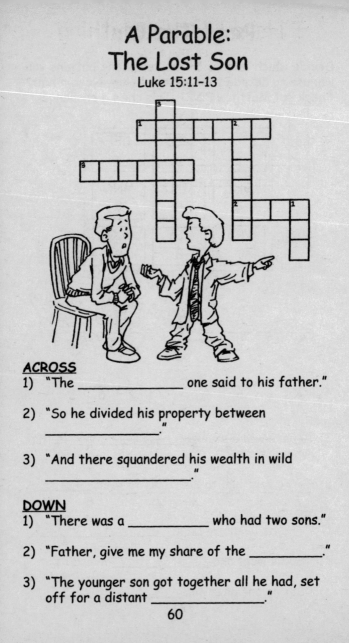

ACROSS

1) "The _____ one said to his father."

2) "So he divided his property between
_____."

3) "And there squandered his wealth in wild
_____."

DOWN

1) "There was a _____ who had two sons."

2) "Father, give me my share of the _____."

3) "The younger son got together all he had, set
off for a distant _____."

I Have Lost Everything
Luke 15:14–16

ACROSS

1) "After he had spent _____."

2) "There was a severe _____ in that whole country."

3) "Who sent him to his fields to feed _____."

DOWN

1) "And he began to be in _____."

2) "So he went and _____ himself out."

3) "But no one gave him _____."

Homebound
Luke 15:17-21

ACROSS

1) "His father saw him and was _____ with compassion."

2) "Father, I have _____ against heaven and against you."

3) "I am no longer _____ to be called your son."

DOWN

1) "I will set out and go back to my _____."

2) "Make me like one of your _____ men."

3) "So he got up and _____ to his father."

My Son Has Returned
Luke 15:20-24

ACROSS

1) "Bring the fattened calf and _____ it."

2) "Bring the best _____ and put it on him."

3) "For this son of mine was dead and is
   _____ again."

DOWN

1) "He ran to his son, threw his arms around him
   and _____ him."

2) "Put a _____ on his finger and
   sandals on his feet."

3) "Let's have a feast and _____."

John's Journey With Jesus
John

1) Who wrote the book of John?

2) Did you know that the book of John does not record the events surrounding Jesus' birth?

3) Where did Jesus perform His first miracle?
    a) Cane   c)   Cana
    b) Cain   d)   Cathy

4) Who told Jesus there was no more wine?

5) The event where Jesus performed His first miracle was a:
    a) circus   c)   wedding
    b) bar mitzvah   d)   birthday
    party

6) Did you know that the author of the Book of John was one of Jesus' twelve disciples?

7) When Jesus saw the money changers at the temple, He:
    a) bought three doves and two goats
    b) asked for change for the vending machines
    c) asked what time the Bible study on the book of Revelation would occur
    d) overturned their tables and angrily rebuked them

8) God promises believers:
    a) earthly riches
    b) eternal life
    c) manna
    d) a year's supply of Rice a Roni, the San Francisco treat

9) What did Jesus ask the woman at the well to give Him?

10) What important news did Jesus tell the woman about Himself?

11) Jesus fed a large crowd of people with:
   a) five barley loaves and two small fish
   b) three cans of soda and a pack of M&Ms
   c) five candy bars and a pint of lemonade
   d) five coffee beans and a peanut butter and jelly sandwich

12) How many people were in the crowd?

13) Jesus was betrayed by:
   a) Judas Iscariot   c) Pharoah
   b) Moses   d) James Bond, Agent 007

14) What did Jesus do to serve His disciples at the Last Supper?

15) What lesson did this teach the disciples?

16) Did you know that Jesus showed He knew who would betray Him by giving Judas bread dipped in wine?

17) Did Jesus know that Peter would deny Him three times?

18) Immediately after Peter had denied Jesus three times, a:
   a) donkey brayed
   b) fire engine siren went off
   c) rooster crowed
   d) woman screamed

19) Did you know that all four Gospels tell us about Peter's denial of Jesus?

20) When Pilate presented Jesus to the mob during Passover, they cried:
    a) He is our king!
    b) Have mercy on Him!
    c) For He's a jolly good fellow!
    d) Crucify Him!

21) What will we do if we love Jesus?

22) What did the sign Pilate made for Jesus' cross say?

23) Did you know that Pilate's sign was written in Aramaic, Greek, and Latin? (John 19:20)

24) What did Jesus say as He died on the cross?

25) The angels at Jesus' tomb said to Mary Magdalene:
    a) Why are you crying?
    b) Fetch us something to eat.
    c) We know you have been married five times.
    d) Why are there so many women named Mary in the Bible?

26) What did the risen Jesus say to Mary Magdalene?

27) Did Thomas believe the other disciples when they said they had seen the risen Christ?

All 'A's
And One 'B'

The first letter to each answer will start with the letter 'A' except one. It will start with the letter 'B'.

1) Who appeared to Joseph in a dream?
   _____ MATT. 1:20

2) The first two apostles (followers of Jesus) were Simon Peter and his brother. MATT. 4:18
   _____

3) Jesus said that we should seek, knock and
   _____ . MATT. 7:7

4) Even though Jesus never did anything wrong, soldiers came to _____ him.
   MARK 14:46

5) After Jesus rose from his death, He came to be with the apostles, and _____ some fish with them. LUKE 24:43

6) These things, in the Bible, are written so that you may _____ in Jesus Christ. JOHN 20:31

What's Your Answer?

Jesus asked His disciples a very important question that is recorded in Mark 8:29. To discover what that question was, begin at the letter **W** on the outside, dark square and skip every other letter.

Peter answered the question. His answer is hidden in the inner square with lighter letters. It begins with the letter Y in the left corner of the inside squares. All of the letters in this answer are next to each other, either diagonally, vertically, or horizontally. Do not skip letters.

Finally, think about how you would answer Jesus' question.

W	A	H	R	O	B	D	K
E	Y	T	S	I	R	H	O
M	H	O	R	G	B	C	Z
P	L	Q	U	W	J	E	Y
A	D	S	X	A	M	H	T
G	I	O	E	N	R	T	O
I	A	P	K	C	F	E	S
E	Y	H	A	R	S	M	U

Jesus' question: _____

_____

Peter's answer: _____

_____

Your answer: _____

_____

68

ACTS

The Book of *Acts* tells what happened when Jesus went to heaven and how Christianity spread to all the world. The *Epistles* are *letters* that the apostles wrote to the new Christians. They help us to understand more about living the Christian life.

Many of the letters were written by Paul. He traveled by ship and on foot and had many exciting adventures telling people about Jesus.

In the puzzle below, x out all the "q"s to find out what Paul wrote to the people of Rome in the book of Romans.

QIQ   QTQHAQNKQ   GQODQ   FQOQR
YQOQU   QAQLQL   QANQDQ
QREQMEQMBQER   QYOQUQQ   QIQNQ
QMQYQ   PQRQAQYQEQRS.

Answer:

_____

_____

_____

_____

_____

_____

_____

News for the Romans
Paul's Epistle to the Romans

1) Who wrote the Epistle to the Romans?

2) The letter was written to:
   a) Roman Christians
   b) Caesar
   c) the owner of Roma Restaurant
   d) the Vatican Council

3) Did you know that the letter to the Romans was written almost sixty years after Jesus was crucified?

4) The letter is written about:
   a) Roman Christians
   b) the Vatican Council
   c) why they should give Paul money for his mission work
   d) God's Son

5) What proof does Paul offer that Jesus is holy?

6) Did you know that the term "saint" applies to any Christian? Paul tells the Roman Christians that they are called to be saints. (Romans 1:7)

7) We can have peace with God through:
   a) random acts of kindness
   b) helping an old lady cross the street every day
   c) making sure we give 10% of our allowance to church every Sunday
   d) faith in our Lord Jesus Christ

8) To receive salvation, we have to pay Jesus:
    a) by being ministers and missionaries when we grow up whether we want to or not
    b) by spending at least an hour a day reading the Bible
    c) by ignoring people who tease us
    d) nothing. His gift of salvation is free.

9) Who makes us righteous?

10) Did you know that the old self Paul talks about is our old nature that wants to sin? (Romans 6:6)

11) Christians live under grace instead of having to follow laws. This is called:
    a) the New Covenant
    b) the Declaration of Independence
    c) the Apostles' Creed
    d) the Girl Scout Pledge

12) Once you stop living for sin, you are guided by:
    a) your minister
    b) your Sunday School teacher
    c) your friends
    d) the Holy Spirit

13) What two things will you find if you live in the Spirit?

14) Is any person righteous without Jesus?

15) When a Christian is too sad or upset to pray, what does the Holy Spirit do?

A Traveling Man

We read a lot about Paul in the New Testament. He traveled to many places preaching the word of God. This puzzle contains the names of some of the cities and towns that he visited on his journeys. All of the clues given below come from the book of Acts. The chapter and verse listed after each statement tell you where you can find the answer in Acts. The word in the vertical box tells you what Paul is called.

1) Where Paul was guarded by a soldier. 28:16

2) Where there was a plot to stone Paul. 14:1-5

3) Where Paul raised a dead man. 20:6-11

4) Where a riot occured. 19:23-32

5) Where Lydia became a Christian. 16:11-15

6) Where Paul told of converting many people. 14:26-28

7) Where Paul got a haircut. 18:18

8) Where people worshiped a lot of idols. 17:16

9) Where Paul was beaten by an angry crowd. 21:30-32

10) Where Paul healed a crippled man. 14:8-10

1) _ _ _|_ _

2) _ _ _ _|_ _ _

3) _ _ _ _|_

4) _ _ _ _|_ _

5) _ _ _ _ _|_ _ _

6) _ _ _ _|_ _

7) _ _ _|_ _ _ _

8) _ _ _|_ _ _

9) _ _ _|_ _ _ _ _

10) _ _|_ _ _ _

"When did Adam and Eve eat the apple?" a Sunday school teacher asked.

"In the summertime," answered a student.

"Why Brenda, how do you know that?" the teacher asked.

"Well, we all know it was just before the fall."

Hebrews

1) Who wrote The Epistle to the Hebrews?

2) Did you know that twenty-one books of the New Testament are epistles?

3) An epistle is a:
    a) letter   c) novel
    b) book   d) wife of an apostle

4) Today, God speaks to us:
    a) through a megaphone
    b) by playing recordings backwards
    c) by appearing in a burning bush
    d) through His Son Jesus

5) Whom does the author of Hebrews trust?

6) As the perfect Son of God, what does Jesus offer to all who obey Him?

7) What are angels?

8) If we accept Jesus, we will find:
    a) a way to make good grades in school
    b) mercy and grace
    c) a lot of money
    d) many friends

9) Good deeds are not as important to the Christian as:
    a) faith
    b) voting
    c) having more video games than anyone else
    d) being the most popular person in school

10) What does God think of good works done in His name?

11) Did you know that today Christians live under the new covenant described in Hebrews? The old Mosaic covenant meant that God's people followed a set of rules. Under the new covenant, Jesus died for our sins. We are forgiven if we accept Jesus as our personal savior. (Hebrews 8:12-13)

12) To please God, a Christian must have:
    a) given up chocolate for Lent
    b) gone to Vacation Bible School every year for five years
    c) a wardrobe of Christian T-shirts and at least 10 CDs by Christian musicians
    d) faith

13) Name at least two people of faith described in Hebrews.

14) Where is Jesus now?

15) What is the last word of the letter to the Hebrews, in the King James Version?

16) Instead of burnt offerings, what sacrifice should we offer to God?

17) God corrects us because He:
    a) will benefit
    b) wants all Christians to be missionaries to the North Pole
    c) wants us to learn how to be holy
    d) thinks it is fun

Answer Pages

PAGE 4: Old Testament Word Find

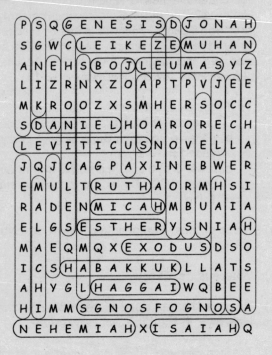

PAGE 6: The Creation and the Fall

1) Moses
2) (Genesis 1:3-5) He separated day and night.
3) (Genesis 1:14-19) the sun, the moon, and the stars
5) (Genesis 2:10) to water the garden
6) (Genesis 2:19) d) Adam
7) (Genesis 2:19) Adam
8) (Genesis 2:18) as a helpmate for Adam
9) (Genesis 3:20) c) Eve
11) (Genesis 2:21) a rib
13) (Genesis 3:1) a) serpent
14) (Genesis 3:5) d) knowledge of good and evil
16) (Genesis 3:7) They sewed themselves aprons made of fig leaves.
17) (Genesis 3:8) They hid themselves.
18) (Genesis 3:12) d) Eve
19) (Genesis 3:22-24) a) sent them out of Eden
20) (Genesis 3:24) cherubim

PAGE 8: Adam and Eve

PAGE 9: Adam and Eve's Sons

PAGE 10: The First Murder—The Flood

1) (Genesis 4:1) Cain
2) (Genesis 4:2) Abel
4) (Genesis 4:16) b) Nod
6) (Genesis 4:25) Seth
7) (Genesis 5:22) Enoch
8) (Genesis 5:22, 24) that he walked with God.
9) (Genesis 5:27) d) 969
10) (Genesis 6:14) c) an ark
12) (Genesis 7:6) 600 years old
13) (Genesis 10:1) a) Ham

PAGE 12: Did It Ever Rain!

1) righteous
2) cypress
3) floodwaters
4) 600
5) wife
6) three, wives
7) 40
8) Ham, Shem, Japheth
9) wind
10) dove

PAGE 13: The Flood

PAGE 14: A New World

1) (Genesis 11:4, 8) c) the Tower of Babel
2) (Genesis 11:7-8) He caused them to speak different languages and scattered them over the earth.
3) (Genesis 13:10) the plain of Jordan
5) (Genesis 16:15) a) the mother of Ishmael
6) (Genesis 16:16) c) 86
7) (Genesis 17:5) b) Abraham
8) (Genesis 17:5) Because He had promised to make him the father of many nations.
10) Moses
11) (Genesis 17:17) d) laughed
12) (Genesis 17:17) because Sarah was very old
13) (Genesis 19:28) a) Sodom and Gomorrah
14) (Genesis 19:26) She turned into a pillar of salt.

PAGE 18: The Blessing

PAGE 19: Batting 1,000
1) Adam lived to be *930*.
2) There were *eight* people in the ark: Noah, Mrs. Noah, their three sons and their wives.
3) There was only *one* language.
4) Joseph had *eleven* brothers.
.5) There are *fifty* chapters in the book of Genesis.

PAGE 20: Strongman Samson
2) (Judges 13:4 and 7) d) wine or strong drink
3) (Judges 13:11-16) a) Samson's father Manoah
4) (Judges 13:18) He didn't say.
5) (Judges 14:3) d) Philistine
6) (Judges 14:5-6) a) killed it with his bare hands
7) (Judges 14:8) c) a swarm of bees and honey
8) (Judges 14:12) He challenged them to solve a riddle.
9) (Judges 14:17) b) Samson's wife
10) (Judges 14:20) a) Samson's friend
11) (Judges 15:16) d) donkey's jawbone
12) (Judges 14:19) He went to the next Philistine town, slew 30 men, and took their cloaks.
13) (Judges 15:19) d) the donkey's jawbone

PAGE 22: From Judges to a King

2) (I Samuel 8:1) b) made his sons judges in his place
3) (I Samuel 8:3) a) took bribes and did not rule fairly
4) (I Samuel 8:2) Joel and Abijah.
5) (I Samuel 8:3) Yes
7) (I Samuel 8:6) b) prayed to the Lord
8) (I Samuel 8:9) a) let the people see how a king would rule
9) (I Samuel 8:7) the Lord Himself
10) (I Samuel 8:10-17) a) greedy
11) (I Samuel 8:19) No. They still wanted a king.
12) Saul
14) (I Samuel 9:2) d) being the tallest and most handsome man in all of Israel

PAGE 24: Young Blood

1) (I Samuel 15:23) because Saul disobeyed God
3) (I Samuel 16:6-7) a) handsome
4) (I Samuel 16:7) d) hearts
5) (I Samuel 16:1) Jesse
6) (I Samuel 16:10) seven
7) (I Samuel 16:12) b) glowing with health and handsome to look at
8) (I Samuel 16:12) The Lord told Samuel to anoint David king.
9) (I Samuel 16:15-17) Because God had sent an evil spirit to bother rebellious Saul.
10) (I Samuel 16:16) d) harp
11) (I Samuel 16:12) David
12) (I Samuel 16:21) a) loved Saul and became his armor-bearer
13) (I Samuel 17:4) a Philistine giant from Gath who taunted the Israelites
15) (I Samuel 17:13) the three eldest brothers, Eliab, Abinadab, and Shammah

PAGE 26: Talking With God: The Psalms

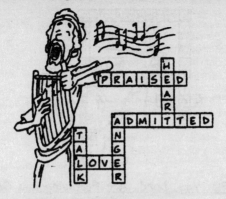

PAGE 27: Majestic Is His Name

PAGE 28: David's Psalm

The Lord is my <u>shepherd</u>, I shall not be in want. He makes me lie down in <u>green</u> <u>pastures</u>, he <u>leads</u> me beside quiet <u>waters</u>, he restores my <u>soul</u>. He guides me in paths of <u>righteousness</u> for his name's sake. Even though I walk through the <u>valley</u> of the <u>shadow</u> of death, I will <u>fear</u> no evil, for you are with me; your <u>rod</u> and your <u>staff</u>, they comfort me. You prepare a table before me in the presence of my enemies. You anoint my <u>head</u> with oil; my <u>cup</u> overflows. Surely goodness and <u>love</u> will follow me all the days of my life, and I will dwell in the <u>house</u> of the Lord <u>forever</u>.

PAGE 29: You, Lord, Are My Salvation

PAGE 30: You, Lord, Are Forgiving and Good

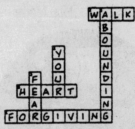

PAGE 32: With God I Will Have Victory

PAGE 34: Proverbs
Yes! You can have:
> The Wisdom of King Solomon.

PAGE 35: Bits of Wisdom
1) (Proverbs 1:1) a) a king of Israel
2) (Proverbs 2:6) the Lord
3) (Proverbs 3:7) d) evil
4) (Proverbs 3:12) a) shows you right from wrong
5) (Proverbs 3:13) wisdom
6) (Proverbs 6:6-8) a) work
7) (Proverbs 6:16) b) seven
8) (Proverbs 6:24) b) bad women
10) (Proverbs 7:4) d) sister
12) (Proverbs 8:11) c) rubies
13) Solomon wrote most of it, although some portions are attributed to others.
15) Wisdom
16) (Proverbs 9:8) b) love you
17) (Proverbs 9:9) Because the wise person is always trying to be wiser. Learning from others is a way to do that.
18) (Proverbs 9:11) Yes
19) (Proverbs 10:12) c) love
20) (Proverbs 11:13) Yes
21) Speaking badly of others is hurtful, and gossip is not always true. Have you ever been hurt by something someone said about you?
22) (Proverbs 13:18) a) poverty and shame
23) (Proverbs 13:18) c) honor
24) (Proverbs 15:1) Give the person a kind answer.

25) (Proverbs 16:24) d) honeycomb
26) (Proverbs 17:6) his grandchildren
27) (Proverbs 19:5) a) tell lies
29) It means that God does not want people to cheat each other. For instance, God would not want a butcher to charge you for two pounds of meat when he is only selling you one.

PAGE 38:
How Can I Make Wise Choices: The Proverbs

PAGE 40: Wisdom Will Save Me

PAGE 41: A Good Name

PAGE 42: The Blessing of the Lord

PAGE 44: The Good Wife
1) (Proverbs 31:10) a) noble
2) A favorable character trait such as
   honesty, charity, thrift, or integrity; Christian behavior.
3) (Proverbs 31:10) rubies
4) (Proverbs 31:11) c) full confidence
5) (Proverbs 31:13) wool and flax
6) (Proverbs 31:28) her husband and children
7) (Proverbs 31:13) c) works willingly
8) (Proverbs 31:14) from far away
9) (Proverbs 31:15) a) before dawn
10) (Proverbs 31:14-19) willingness to work; the work ethic

11) (Proverbs 31:20) d) charity
12) (Proverbs 31:21) b) she has plenty of clothing to keep her family warm
13) (Proverbs 31:22) purple
15) (Proverbs 31:24) fine linen
16) (Proverbs 31:25) d) strength and dignity
17) (Proverbs 31:26) wisdom
18) (Proverbs 31:30) c) is not vain or conceited

PAGE 46: Dream Weaver

1) Daniel
3) (Daniel 1:8) d) to be excused from eating food forbidden under Jewish dietary laws
4) (Daniel 1:9) favor and compassion
5) (Daniel 1:17) understanding of visions and dreams
7) (Daniel 2:12) that they all should be killed
8) (Daniel 3:1) gold
10) (Daniel 2:16-18) a) asked the king for more time and prayed to God for wisdom
11) (Daniel 3:6) c) thrown into a fiery furnace
12) (Daniel 4:32-33) a) went to live with the beasts of the field, eating grass for food
14) (Daniel 5:4) He praised other gods.
15) (Daniel 5:5) a) with handwriting on a wall

PAGE 48: The Unwilling Servant

1) Jonah
3) (Jonah 1:2) Nineveh
4) (Jonah 1:3) c) Joppa
5) (Jonah 1:3) b) on a ship heading to Tarshish
7) (Jonah 1:4) a great wind
8) (Jonah 1:5) a) their gods
9) (Jonah 1:13) No. They tried to row to land first, but failed because of the rough waters.
11) (Jonah 1:12) d) throw him overboard
12) (Jonah 1:15) d) grew calm
13) (Jonah 2:1) He prayed.
14) (Jonah 3:1-2) b) go to Nineveh
16) (Jonah 1:17) three days and three nights
17) (Jonah 3:4) that Nineveh would be overthrown in forty days
18) (Jonah 3:5) a) fasted and wore sackcloth

```
F  B  E  A  R  E  N
B  R  A  B  B  I  T
M  J  A  C  K  A  L
L  A  S  D  O  G  P
V  S  H  E  E  P  O
G  R  E  F  R  O  G
C  E  A  G  L  E  N
P  S  T  H  A  R  E
B  L  P  I  G  N  I
         J

C  O  C  K  E  R  G
S  M  O  L  E  N  A
T  R  E  M  O  T  H
L  I  O  N  B  R  O
D  U  G  O  A  T  L
L  E  O  P  A  R  D
         Q

S  P  A  R  R  O  W
M  O  U  S  E  A  C
R  B  A  T  T  L  V
M  O  Q  U  A  I  L
G  D  O  V  E  L  I
S  N  O  W  L  E  R
T  F  O  X  E  N  Z
         Y

S  L  I  Z  A  R  D
```

PAGE 52: New Testament Word Find

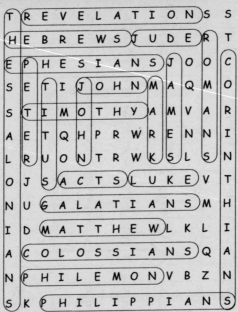

PAGE 54: Matthew's Gospel

1) Matthew
3) d) Jesus' birth line, or genealogy
5) (Matthew 2:1) Bethlehem
7) (Matthew 2:13) d) kill Him
8) (Matthew 2:13) a) Egypt
9) (Matthew 3:4) d) locusts and wild honey
11) (Matthew 4:2) forty days and forty nights
12) (Matthew 4:19) men (or people)
13) a) Beatitudes
15) (Matthew 6:9-13) the Lord's Prayer
16) (Matthew 6:20) d) heaven
18) (Matthew 7:12) the Golden Rule
19) (Matthew 8:14) d) mother-in-law
20) parables
21) (Matthew 10:1) twelve
22) (Matthew 14:26) a) ghost
23) (Matthew 15:28) a) great faith

24) (Matthew 20:17-19) Yes
25) (Matthew 24:42) b) we don't know when the Lord will
    return
26) (Matthew 26:14-15) Judas Iscariot
27) (Matthew 26:15) d) thirty pieces of silver
28) (Matthew 26:36) the Garden of Gethsemane

PAGE 57: A Parable: The Lost Sheep

PAGE 58: I Was Lost, But Now I'm Found

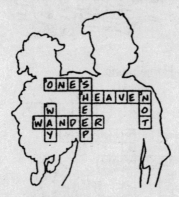

PAGE 59: Read the Dial

Well done, good and faithful servant!

PAGE 60: A Parable: The Lost Son

PAGE 61: I Have Lost Everything

PAGE 62: Homebound

PAGE 63: My Son Has Returned

PAGE 64: John's Journey With Jesus

1) John
3) (John 2:1) c) Cana
4) (John 2:3) His mother
5) (John 2:1) c) wedding
7) (John 2:15) d) overturned their tables and angrily rebuked them
8) (John 3:16) b) eternal life
9) (John 4:7) a drink of water
10) (John 4:26) That He is the Messiah.
11) (John 6:9) a) five barley loaves and two small fish
12) (John 6:10) 5000
13) (John 12:4) a) Judas Iscariot
14) (John 13:14) He washed their feet.
15) (John 13:14) to serve one another
17) (John 13:38) Yes
18) (John 18:27) c) rooster crowed
20) (John 19:15) d) Crucify Him!
21) (John 14:15) We will keep His commandments.
22) (John 19:19) Jesus of Nazareth, the King of the Jews
24) (John 19:30) It is finished.
25) (John 20:13) a) Why are you crying?
26) (John 20:15) Woman, why are you crying?
27) (John 20:25) No. He wanted proof.

PAGE 67: All 'A's And One 'B'

Did you find them all?

1) Angel
2) Andrew
3) Ask
4) Arrest
5) Ate
6) Believe

PAGE 68: What's Your Answer?

Jesus' question: Who do you say I am?
Peter's answer: You are the Christ.

PAGE 69: Acts

Paul wrote:

I thank God for you all and remember you in my prayers.

PAGE 70: News for the Romans

1) Paul the Apostle
2) (Romans 1:7) a) Roman Christians
4) (Romans 1:3) d) God's Son
5) (Romans 1:4) Jesus' resurrection from the dead
7) (Romans 5:1) d) faith in our Lord Jesus Christ
8) (Romans 5:18) d) nothing. His gift of salvation is free.
9) (Romans 5:21) Jesus Christ, the Son of God
11) (Hebrews 8:13) a) the New Covenant
12) (Romans 8:1-2) d) the Holy Spirit
13) (Romans 8:6) life and peace
14) (Romans 3:10) No
15) (Romans 8:26) The Holy Spirit tells God what the Christian needs.

PAGE 72: A Traveling Man

```
1.            R  O  M  E
2.      I  C  O  N  I  U  M
3.      T  R  O  A  S
4.      E  P  H  E  S  U  S
5.      P  H  I  L  I  P  P  I
6.      A  N  T  I  O  C  H
7.            C  E  N  C  H  R  E  A
8.                  A  T  H  E  N  S
9.         J  E  R  U  S  A  L  E  M
10.            L  Y  S  T  R  A
```

PAGE 74: Hebrews

1) We do not know, although some Bible scholars think Paul the Apostle wrote it.
3) a) letter
4) (Hebrews 1:1-2) d) through His Son Jesus
5) (Hebrews 2:13) Jesus
6) (Hebrews 5:8-9) eternal salvation; everlasting life
7) (Hebrews 1:14) ministering spirits
8) (Hebrews 4:16) b) mercy and grace
9) (Hebrews 6:1) a) faith
10) (Hebrews 6:10) He will not forget them.
12) (Hebrews 11:6) d) faith
13) (Hebrews 11) Abel, Enoch, Noah, Abraham, Sarah, Isaac, Jacob, Joseph, the parents of Moses, Moses, Rahab
14) (Hebrews 12:2) He sits at the right hand of the throne of God.
15) Amen.
16) (Hebrews 13:15) continual praise
17) (Hebrews 12:10) c) wants us to learn how to be holy

LIKE JOKES OR TRIVIA?

Then check out these great books from
Barbour Publishing!